To _____

From _____

Published by Simple Truths, LLC
1952 McDowell Road, Suite 205
Naperville, IL 60563

Cover Photo: Bruce Heinemann
Design: Rich Nickel
Editor: Jennifer Svoboda

Printed and bound in China

www.simpletruths.com

02 4CPG 10

The STRANGEST SECRET

HOW TO LIVE THE LIFE YOU DESIRE

EARL NIGHTINGALE

Some years ago, the late Nobel Prize-winner Dr. Albert Schweitzer was being interviewed in London, and a reporter asked him, "Doctor, what's wrong with men today?" The great doctor was silent a moment, and then he said, "Men simply don't think!"

It's about this that I want to talk with you.

We live today in a golden age. This is an era that humanity has looked forward to, dreamed of, and worked toward for thousands of years, but since it's here, we pretty well take it for granted. We in America are particularly fortunate to live in the richest land that ever existed on the face of the earth...a land of abundant opportunity for everyone.

However, if you take 100 individuals who start even at the age of 25, do you have any idea what will happen to those men and women by the time they're 65? These 100 people who all start even at the age of 25 believe they're going to be successful. If you asked any one of these people if they wanted to be a success, they would tell you they did…and you'd notice that they were eager toward life, that there was a certain sparkle in their eye, an erectness to their carriage, and life seemed like a pretty interesting adventure to them.

But by the time they're 65,
one will be rich,
four will be financially independent,
five will still be working and
54 will be broke.

So, of 100, only five make the grade! Why do so many fail? What has happened to the sparkle that was there when they were 25? What has become of the dreams, the hopes, the plans...and why is there such a large disparity between what these people intended to do and what they actually accomplished?

When we say about five percent achieve success, we have to define success. Here is the best definition I've ever been able to find:

"*Success is the progressive*

If someone is working toward a predetermined goal, and knows where he or she is going, that person is a success. If they are not doing that, they are failures. *"Success is the progressive realization of a worthy ideal."*

realization of a worthy ideal."

Rollo May, the distinguished psychiatrist, wrote a wonderful book called *Man's Search for Himself,* and in this book, he says, "The opposite of courage in our society is not cowardice…it is conformity."

And there you have the trouble today: conformity — people acting like everyone else… without knowing why or where they are going.

In America right now, there are over 25 million people 65 years of age and older…and most of them are broke; they're dependent on someone else for life's necessities.

We learn to read by the time we're seven. We learn to make a living by the time we're 25. Usually by that time we're not only making a living, we're supporting a family. And yet by the time we're 65, we haven't learned how to become financially independent in the richest land that has ever been known. Why? We conform!

The trouble is that we're acting like the wrong percentage group - the 95 who don't succeed.

Why do these people conform? Well, they really don't know. These people believe that their lives are shaped by circumstances…by things that happen to them…by exterior forces. They're outer-directed people.

A survey was made of working people and they were asked, "Why do you work? Why do you get up in the morning?" Nineteen out of 20 had no idea. If you ask them, they would say, "Well, everybody goes to work in the morning." And that's the reason they do it — because everyone else is doing it.

Now, let's get back to our definition of success. Who succeeds?

The only person who succeeds is the person who is progressively realizing a worthy ideal. He's the person who says,

"I'm going to become this"
...and then begins to work
toward that goal.

*A success is —*

– the school teacher who is teaching school because that's what he or she wants to do.

– the woman who is a wife and mother because she wanted to become a wife and mother and is doing a good job of it.

– the entrepreneur who starts his own company because that was his dream — that's what he wanted to do.

– the salesperson who wants to become a topnotch salesperson and grow and build with his or her organization.

*Instead of competing,
all we have to do is create!*

A success is anyone who is doing deliberately a predetermined job, because that's what he or she decided to do…deliberately. But only one out of 20 does that!

That's why today there isn't really any competition, unless we make it for ourselves. Instead of competing, all we have to do is create!

For 20 years, I looked for the key which would determine what would happen to a human being. Was there a key, I wanted to know, which would make the future a promise that we could foretell to a larger extent? Was there a key that would guarantee a person's becoming successful if he or she only knew about it and knew how to use it?

Well, there is such a key, and I've found it.

Have you ever wondered why so many people work so hard and honestly without ever achieving anything in particular, and others don't seem to work hard, yet seem to get everything? They seem to have the magic touch. You've heard people say, "Everything he touches turns to gold." And have you ever noticed that a person who becomes successful tends to continue to become more successful — and, on the other hand, have you noticed how someone who's a failure tends to continue to fail?

Well, it's because of goals. People with goals succeed because they know where they're going. It's that simple.

Think of a ship leaving a harbor. And think of it with the complete voyage mapped out and planned. The captain and crew know exactly where the ship is going and how long it will take — it has a definite goal. And 9,999 times out of 10,000, it will get there.

Now let's take another ship — just like the first — only let's not put a crew on it, or a captain at the helm. Let's give it no aiming point, no goal, and no destination. We just start the engines and let it go. I think you'll agree that if it gets out of the harbor at all, it will either sink or wind up on some deserted beach — a derelict. It can't go anyplace, because it has no destination and no guidance.

It's the same with a human being.

Take the salesperson, for example. There is no other person in the world today with the future of a good salesperson. Selling is the world's highest-paid profession — if we're good at it, and if we know where we're going. Every company needs topnotch salespeople, and they reward those people. The sky is the limit for them. But how many can you find?

Someone once said that the human race is fixed, not to prevent the strong from winning, but to prevent the weak from losing.

The American economy today can be likened to a convoy in time of war. The entire economy is slowed down to protect its weakest link, just as the convoy has to go at the speed that will permit its slowest vessel to remain in formation.

That's why it's so easy to make a living today. It takes no particular brains or talent to make a living and support a family. So we have a plateau of so-called "security", if that's what a person is looking for. But we do have to decide how high above this plateau we want to aim.

We have to decide how high above this plateau we want to aim.

Now let's get back to The Strangest Secret, the story that I wanted to tell you today. And I'd like to begin by asking you an extremely important question:

Why do people with goals succeed in life… and people without them fail?

Well, let me tell you something that, if you really understand it, will alter your life immediately. If you understand completely what I'm going to tell you, from this moment on, your life will never be the same again. You'll suddenly find that good luck just seems to be attracted to you. The things you want just seem to fall in line. And from now on you won't have the problems, the worries, the gnawing lump of anxiety that perhaps you've experienced before. Doubt…fear…well, they'll be things of the past.

We become what
we think about.

Here's the key to success and the key to failure: We become what we think about. Now, let me repeat that. *We become what we think about.*

Throughout all history, the great wise men and teachers, philosophers, and prophets have disagreed with one another on many different things. It is only on this one point that they are in complete and unanimous agreement.

Consider what Marcus Aurelius, the great Roman Emperor, said:

"A man's life is what his thoughts make of it."

Benjamin Disraeli said this: "Everything comes if a man will only wait. I have brought myself by long meditation to the conviction that a human being with a settled purpose must accomplish it, and that nothing can resist a will that will stake even existence for its fulfillment."

Ralph Waldo Emerson said this:

"A man is what he thinks about all day long."

William James said: "The greatest discovery of my generation is that human beings can alter their lives by altering their attitudes of mind."

And he also said: "We need only in cold blood act as if the thing in question were real, and it will become infallibly real by growing into such a connection with our life that it will become real. It will become so knit with habit and emotion that our interests in it will be those which characterize belief."

He also said: "If you only care enough for a result, you will almost certainly attain it. If you wish to be rich, you will be rich; if you wish to be learned, you will be learned; if you wish to be good, you will be good. Only you must, then, really wish these things, and wish them exclusively, and not wish at the same time a hundred other incompatible things just as strongly."

"*Human beings can alter their lives by altering their attitudes of mind.*"

Believe and Succeed

In the Bible, you'll read in Mark 9:23: "If thou canst believe, all things are possible to him that believeth."

My old friend, Dr. Norman Vincent Peale, put it this way: "This is one of the greatest laws in the universe, fervently do I wish I had discovered it as a very young man. It dawned upon me much later in life, and I have found it to be one of my greatest — if not my greatest — discovery, outside of my relationship to God…The great law briefly and simply stated is that if you think in negative terms, you will get negative results. If you think in positive terms, you will achieve positive results." "That is the simple fact," he went on to say, "which is the basis of an astonishing law of prosperity and success. In three words: Believe and Succeed."

William Shakespeare put it this way:

"Our doubts are traitors, and make us lose the good we oft might win, by fearing to attempt."

George Bernard Shaw said, "People are always blaming their circumstances for what they are. I don't believe in circumstances. The people who get on in this world are the people who get up and look for the circumstances they want, and if they can't find them, make them."

Well, it's pretty apparent, isn't it? And every person who discovered this believed (for a while) that he was the first one to work it out. We become what we think about.

Now, it stands to reason that a person who is thinking about a concrete and worthwhile goal is going to reach it, because that's what he's thinking about. And we become what we think about.

Conversely, the person who has no goal, who doesn't know where he's going, and whose thoughts must therefore be thoughts of confusion, anxiety, fear and worry — his life becomes one of frustration, fear, anxiety and worry. And if he thinks about nothing...he becomes nothing.

We become what
we think about.

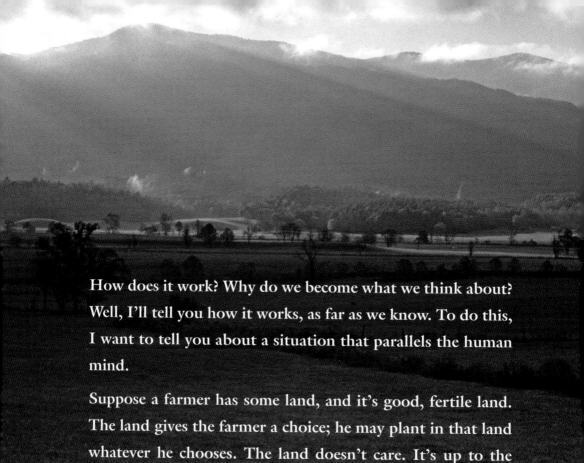

How does it work? Why do we become what we think about? Well, I'll tell you how it works, as far as we know. To do this, I want to tell you about a situation that parallels the human mind.

Suppose a farmer has some land, and it's good, fertile land. The land gives the farmer a choice; he may plant in that land whatever he chooses. The land doesn't care. It's up to the farmer to make the decision.

We're comparing the human mind with the land because the mind, like the land, doesn't care what you plant in it. It will return what you plant, but it doesn't care what you plant.

Now, let's say that the farmer has two seeds in his hand — one is a seed of corn, the other is nightshade, a deadly poison. He digs two little holes in the earth and he plants both seeds — one corn, the other nightshade. He covers up the holes, waters and takes care of the land...and what will happen? Invariably, the land will return what was planted. As it's written in the Bible,

"As ye sow, so shall ye reap."

The human mind is
the last great, unexplored
continent on earth.

Remember, the land doesn't care. It will return poison in just as wonderful abundance as it will corn. So up come the two plants — one corn, one poison.

The human mind is far more fertile, far more incredible and mysterious than the land, but it works the same way. It doesn't care what we plant...success...or failure. A concrete, worthwhile goal...or confusion, misunderstanding, fear, anxiety, and so on. But what we plant it must return to us.

You see, the human mind is the last great, unexplored continent on earth. It contains riches beyond our wildest dreams. It will return anything we want to plant.

Now, you might say, if that's true, why don't people use their minds more? Well, I think they've figured out an answer to that one, too. Our mind comes as standard equipment at birth. It's free. And things that are given to us for nothing, we place little value on. Things that we pay money for, we value.

The paradox is that exactly the reverse is true.

Everything that's really worthwhile in life came to us free — our minds, our souls, our bodies, our hopes, our dreams, our ambitions, our intelligence, our love of family and children and friends and country.

All these priceless possessions are free.

*The things
we get for
nothing,
we can never
replace.*

But the things that cost us money are actually very cheap and can be replaced at any time. A good man can be completely wiped out and make another fortune. He can do that several times. Even if our home burns down, we can rebuild it. But the things we got for nothing, we can never replace.

The human mind isn't used because we take it for granted. Familiarity breeds contempt. It can do any kind of job we assign to it, but generally speaking, we use it for little jobs instead of big ones. Universities have proven that most of us are operating on about 10 percent or less of our abilities.

So decide now. What is it you want? Plant your goal in your mind. It's the most important decision you'll ever make in your entire life.

What is it you want? Do you want to be an outstanding salesperson? A better worker at your particular job? Do you want to go places in your company...in your community? Do you want to get rich?

All you have got to do is plant that seed in your mind, care for it, work steadily toward your goal, and it will become a reality.

It not only will, there's no way that it cannot. You see, that's a law — like the laws of Sir Isaac Newton, the laws of gravity. If you get on top of a building and jump off, you'll always go down — you'll never go up.

And it's the same with all the other laws of nature. They always work. They're inflexible.

Think about your goal in a relaxed, positive way.

Picture yourself in your mind's eye as having already achieved this goal. See yourself doing the things you will be doing when you have reached your goal.

Ours has been called the "Phenobarbital Age", the age of ulcers, nervous breakdowns and tranquilizers. At a time when medical research has raised us to new plateau of good health and longevity, far too many of us worry ourselves into an early grave trying to cope with things in our own little personal ways — without ever learning a few great laws that will take care of everything for us.

These things we bring on ourselves through our habitual way of thinking. Every one of us is the sum total of our own thoughts. We are where we are because that's exactly where we really want to be — whether we'll admit that or not.

Each of us must live off the fruit of our thoughts in the future, because what you think today and tomorrow — next month and next year — will mold your life and determine your future.

You're guided by your mind.

We must control our thinking.

I remember one time I was driving through eastern Arizona and I saw one of those giant earth-moving machines roaring along the road at about 35 miles an hour with what looked like 30 tons of dirt in it...a tremendous, incredible machine...and there was a little man perched way up on top with the wheel in his hands, guiding it. And as I drove along, I was struck by the similarity of that machine to the human mind. Just suppose you're sitting at the controls of such a vast source of energy.

Are you going to sit back and fold your arms and let it run itself into a ditch? Or are you going to keep both hands firmly on the wheel and control and direct this power to a specific, worthwhile purpose? It's up to you. You're in the driver's seat. You see, the very law that gives us success is a two-edged sword. We must control our thinking. The same rule that can lead people to lives of success, wealth, happiness, and all the things they ever dreamed of for themselves and their families — that very same law can lead them into the gutter. It's all in how they use it...for good or for bad. This is The Strangest Secret!

Life should be an exciting adventure.

Now, why do I say it's strange, and why do I call it a secret? Actually, it isn't a secret at all. It was first revealed by some of the earliest wise men, and it appears again and again throughout the Bible. But very few people have learned it or understand it. That's why it's strange, and why for some equally strange reason it virtually remains a secret. I believe that you could go out and walk down the main street of your town and ask one person after another what the secret of success is and you probably wouldn't run into one person in a month who could tell you.

Now, this information is enormously valuable to us, if we really understand it and apply it. It's valuable to us not only for our own lives, but the lives of those around us — our families, employees, associates, and friends.

Life should be an exciting adventure; it should never be a bore. *You should live fully — be alive.*

You should be glad to get out of bed in the morning. You should be doing a job you like to do and because you do it well.

One time I heard Grove Patterson, the great, late editor-in-chief of the *Toledo Daily Blade*, make a speech. And as he concluded his speech he said something I've never forgotten. He said, "My years in the newspaper business have convinced me of several things. Among them, that people are basically good and that we came from someplace and we're going someplace. So we should make our time here an exciting adventure."

"The architect of the universe didn't build a stairway leading nowhere."

And the greatest teacher of all, the carpenter from the plains of Galilee, gave us the secret time and time again, "As ye believe, so shall it be done unto you."

I've explained what I call The Strangest Secret and how it works. Now I want to explain how you can prove to yourself the enormous returns possible in your own life by putting this secret to a practical test. I want to make a test that will last 30 days. It isn't going to be easy but if you will give it a good try,

it will completely change your life for the better.

Back in the seventeenth century, Sir Isaac Newton, the English mathematician and philosopher, gave us some natural laws of physics which apply as much to human beings as they do to the movement of bodies in the universe. And one of these laws is that for every action, there is an equal and opposite reaction. Simply stated, as it applies to you and me, it means we can achieve nothing without paying the price. The results of your 30-day experiment will be in direct proportion to the effort you put forth.

To be a doctor, you must pay the price of long years of difficult study. To be successful in selling — and remember that each of us succeeds to the extent of his ability to sell; selling our families on our ideas, selling education in schools, selling our children on the advantages of living the good and honest life, selling our associates and employees on the importance of being exceptional people...also, of course, the profession of selling itself — to be successful in selling our way to the good life,

we must be willing to pay the price.

Now, what is that price?

Well, it's many things:

First, it's understanding emotionally as well as intellectually that we literally become what we think about; that we must control our thoughts if we're to control our lives. It's understanding fully that... "as ye sow, so shall ye reap."

Second, it's cutting away all fetters from the mind and permitting it to soar as it was divinely designed to do. It's the realization that your limitations are self-imposed and that the opportunities for you today are enormous beyond belief. It's rising above narrow-minded pettiness and prejudice.

Third, it's using all your courage to force yourself to think positively on your own problems; to set a definite and clearly defined goal for yourself. To let your marvelous mind think about your goal from all possible angles; to let your imagination speculate freely upon many different possible solutions. To refuse to believe that there are any circumstances sufficiently strong enough to defeat you in the accomplishment of your purpose. To act promptly and decisively when your course is clear. And to keep constantly aware of the fact that you are, at this moment, standing in the middle of your own "acre of diamonds," as Russell Conwell used to point out.

And fourth, save at least 10 percent of every dollar you earn.

It's also remembering that, no matter what your present job, it has enormous possibilities — if you're willing to pay the price by keeping these four points in mind:

1. *You will become what you think about.*

2. *Remember the word "imagination" and let your mind begin to soar.*

3. *Courageously concentrate on your goal every day.*

4. *Save 10 percent of what you earn.*

Finally, *take action* — ideas are worthless unless we act on them.

Now, I'll try to outline the 30-day test I want you to take. Keep in mind that you have nothing to lose by taking this test…and everything you could possibly want to gain.

There are two things that may be said of everyone: Each of us wants something. And each of us is afraid of something.

I want you to write on a card what it is you want more that anything else.

It may be more money. Perhaps you'd like to double your income or make a specific amount of money. It may be a beautiful home. It may be success at your job. It may be a particular position in life. It could be a more harmonious family.

*Abundance is yours
for the asking.*

Each of us wants something. Write down on your card specifically what it is you want. Make sure it's a single goal and clearly defined. You needn't show it to anyone, but carry it with you so that you can look at it several times a day. Think about it in a cheerful, relaxed, positive way each morning when you get up, and immediately

you have something to work for...
something to get out of bed for...
something to live for.

Look at it every chance you get during the day and just before going to bed at night. And as you look at it, remember that you must become what you think about, and since you're thinking about your goal, you realize that soon it will be yours. In fact, it's really yours the moment you write it down and begin to think about it.

Look at the abundance all around you as you go about your daily business. You have as much right to this abundance as any other living creature. It's yours for the asking.

Now we come to the difficult part — difficult because it means the formation of what is probably a brand new habit, and new habits are not easily formed. Once formed, however, it will follow you for the rest of your life.

Stop thinking about what it is you fear. Each time a fearful or negative thought comes into your consciousness, replace it with a mental picture of your positive and worthwhile goal. And there will come a time when you'll feel like giving up. It's easier for a human being to think negatively than positively. That's why only five percent are successful. You must begin now to place yourself in that group.

For 30 days, you must take control of your mind. It will think only about what you permit it to think about.

All you have to do is

Each day for this 30-day test do more than you have to do. In addition to maintaining a cheerful, positive outlook, give of yourself more than you have ever done before. Do this knowing that your returns in life must be in direct proportion to what you give.

The moment you decide on a goal to work toward, you're immediately a successful person. You are then in that rare and successful category of people who know where they're going. Out of every hundred people, you belong in the top five. Don't concern yourself too much with how you are going to achieve your goal — leave that completely to a power greater than yourself. All you have to do is know where you're going. The answers will come to you of their own accord, and at the right time.

know where you're going.

Remember these words from the Sermon on the Mount, and remember them well. Keep them constantly before you during this month of your test:

"Ask, and it shall be given you;
seek, and ye shall find;
knock, and it shall be opened unto you.
For everyone that asketh receiveth;
and he that seeketh findeth;
and to him that knocketh
it shall be opened."

It's as marvelous and as simple as that. In fact, it's so simple that in our seemingly complicated world, it's difficult for an adult to understand that all he or she needs is a purpose…and faith!

For 30 days, do your very best.

No matter what your job, do it as you've never done it before for 30 days, and — if you've kept your goal before you every day — you'll wonder and marvel at this new life you've found.

Dorothea Brande, the outstanding editor and writer, discovered it for herself and tells about it in her fine book *Wake Up and Live*. Her entire philosophy is reduced to the words: "Act as though it were impossible to fail."

She made her own test, with sincerity and faith, and her entire life was changed to one of overwhelming success.

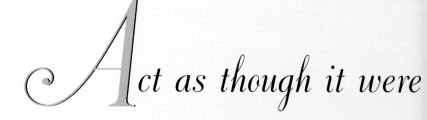

Act as though it were

impossible to fail.

Now, you make your test…for 30 full days. Don't start your test until you've made up your mind to stick with it. You see, by being persistent, you're demonstrating faith; persistence is simply another word for faith. If you didn't have faith, you would never persist.

If you should fail during your first 30 days — by that I mean suddenly find yourself overwhelmed by negative thoughts — you've got to start over again from that point and go 30 more days. Gradually, your new habit will form, until you find yourself one of that wonderful minority to whom virtually

nothing is impossible.

And don't forget the card. It's vitally important as you begin this new way of living. On one side of the card write your goal, whatever it may be. On the other side write these words: "You become what you think about."

In your spare time during your test period, read books that will help you. Inspirational books like Dorothea Brand's *Wake Up and Live* (if you can still find a copy); *The Magic of Believing,* by Claude Bristol; the *Bible; Think and Grow Rich,* by Napoleon Hill; and any other books that instruct and inspire. Nothing great was ever accomplished without inspiration. See that during these crucial first 30 days, your own inspiration is kept at a peak.

Above all...don't worry! Worry brings fear, and fear is crippling. The only thing that can cause you to worry during your test is trying to do it all yourself. Know that all you have to do is hold your goal before you; everything else will take care of itself.

Remember also to keep calm and cheerful. Don't let petty things annoy you and get you off course.

Remember to keep calm and cheerful.

Now, since taking this test is difficult, some may say, "Why should I bother?" Well, look at the alternative! No one wants to be a failure; no one really wants to be a mediocre individual; no one wants a life constantly filled with worry, fear, and frustration.

Therefore, remember that you must reap that which you sow. If you sow negative thoughts, your life will be filled with negative things. If you sow positive thoughts, your life will be cheerful, successful, and positive.

Gradually, you will have a tendency to forget what you've read in this book. Read it often; keep reminding yourself of what you must do to form this new habit. Gather your whole family around at regular intervals and review what's been written here.

Most people will tell you that they want to make money, without understanding this law. The only people who make money work in a mint. The rest of us must earn money. This is what causes those who keep looking for something for nothing, or a free ride, to fail in life.

The only way to earn money is by providing people with services or products which are needed and useful. We exchange our time and our product or service for the other person's money. Therefore, the law is that our financial return will be in direct proportion to our service.

Now, success is not the result of making money; making money is the result of success — and success is in direct proportion to our service.

Most people have this law backwards. They believe that you're successful if you earn a lot of money. The truth is that you can only earn money after you're successful.

Be of service…build…

It's like the story of the man who sat in front of the stove and said to it: "Give me heat and then I'll add the wood."

work...dream...create!

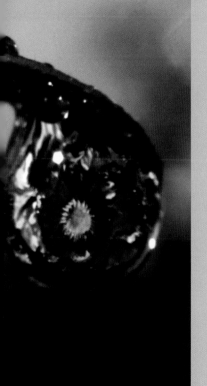

How many men and women do you know, or do you suppose there are today, who take the same attitude toward life? There are millions.

We've got to put the fuel in before we can expect heat. Likewise, we've got to be of service first before we can expect money. Don't concern yourself with the money. Be of service...build...work...dream...create! Do this and you'll find there is no limit to the prosperity and abundance that will come to you.

Prosperity, you know, is founded upon a law of mutual exchange. Any person who contributes to prosperity must prosper, in turn, himself. Sometimes the return will not come from those you serve, but it must come to you from someplace because that's the law.

For every action there is an equal and opposite reaction.

As you go daily through your 30-day test period, remember that your success will always be measured by the quality and quantity of service you render, and money is a yardstick for measuring this service.

*No man can get rich himself
unless he enriches others.*

There are no exceptions to this law. You can drive down any street in America and from your car estimate the service that is being rendered by the people living on that street. Had you ever thought of this yardstick before? It's interesting. Some, like ministers and priests and other devoted people, measure their returns in the realm of the spiritual, but again, their returns are equal to their service.

Once this law is fully understood, any thinking person can tell his own fortune. If he wants more, he must be of more service to those from whom he receives his return. If he wants less, he has only to reduce this service. This is the price you must pay for what you want.

If you believe you can enrich yourself by deluding others, you can end only by deluding yourself. It may take some time, but just as surely as you breathe, you'll get back what you put out. Don't ever make the mistake of thinking you can avert this. It's impossible!

The prisons and the streets where the lonely walk are filled with people who tried to make new laws just for themselves. We may avoid the laws of man for a while. But there are greater laws that cannot be broken.

An outstanding medical doctor once pointed out six steps that will help you realize success:

1. *Set yourself a definite goal.*

2. *Quit running yourself down.*

3. *Stop thinking of all the reasons why you cannot be successful, and instead, think of all the reasons why you can.*

4. *Trace your attitudes back through your childhood, and try to discover where you first got the idea you couldn't be successful, if that's the way you've been thinking.*

5. *Change the image you have of yourself by writing out a description of the person you would like to be.*

6. *Act the part of the successful person you have decided to become!*

The doctor who wrote those words is the noted West Coast psychiatrist, Dr. David Harold Fink.

Do what experts since the dawn of recorded history have told you you must do: pay the price by becoming the person you want to become. It's not nearly as difficult as living unsuccessfully.

Take your 30-day test, then repeat it…then repeat it again. Each time it will become more a part of you until you'll wonder how you could have ever have lived any other way. Live this new way and the floodgates of abundance will open and pour over you more riches than you may have dreamed existed. Money? Yes, lots of it.

But what's more important, you'll have peace… you'll be in that wonderful minority who lead calm, cheerful, successful lives.

Start today. You have nothing to lose — but you have a whole life to win.

This is Earl Nightingale…and thank you.

You have a whole life to win.

SIMPLE TRUTHS

ABOUT THE PUBLISHER

_____

At Simple Truths, we believe that your core values will determine your success in business and life. That is our reason for being. In fact, our goal, like our name, is simple… to help you, or your company, reinforce what's most important and to show that you care.

If you have enjoyed this book and wish to learn more about our full line of beautifully-designed gift books, please visit us at www.simpletruths.com.

There you'll find not only our great gift books, but also many packaging and personalization options to fit your needs as well. Our product themes include *Leadership, Customer Service, Teamwork, Attitude, Selling, Success* and many others.

TEN WAYS TO USE OUR PRODUCTS

➤ *A meeting or convention gift to reinforce your theme.*

➤ *An employee birthday gift sent to their home.*

➤ *An employee anniversary gift sent to their home.*

➤ *A thank you for "going the extra mile."*

➤ *A gift to celebrate a company milestone (i.e., anniversary, reaching a sales goal).*

➤ *A year-end "thanks for your business" gift.*

➤ *A gift to celebrate your company's anniversary (every five years).*

➤ *A "first order" thank you gift.*

➤ *A "leave behind" or "thank you" gift for salespeople.*

➤ *A gift to your best prospects saying, "I'm still here, and I still care."*

To speak to one of our customer service representatives or
to order our Simple Truths catalog, please call 800-900-3427
or visit **www.simpletruths.com**

IT'S TIME FOR YOU TO…
LEAD THE FIELD

*H*undreds of thousands of people have profited from
the wisdom and savvy of Earl Nightingale's *Lead the Field.*
In fact, it has often been referred to as "the program of presidents"
because so many top executives incorporate Nightingale's guidance
and wisdom into their management philosophies.

*W*hen you listen to this landmark program, you'll be awestruck by the simplicity and timelessness of Earl Nightingale's words and ideas. You'll learn the biggest stumbling block to high achievement — and how easy it is to overcome. Through your repeated listening, this treasure trove of insightful information will teach you, among many other things:

> *How to develop a good attitude*

> *Ways to control how others feel about you*

> *Two extremely important words (Hint: The first is gratitude)*

> *The importance of forgiveness*

> *Why duty should bring you joy*

> *Five reminders that will put you in the driver's seat*

> *The usefulness of constructive discontent*

Lead the Field has changed thousands of lives, brought about extraordinary success, and helped create multi-millionaires around the world.

Now it's your turn. With *The Strangest Secret*, you have already taken the first step toward the life you most desire. Don't stop here.
Take the next step and *Lead the Field.*   Call **1-800-535-2751**
or visit **www.nightingale.com/SimpleTruths** today.

PHOTO CREDITS